DISCARD

c. 1

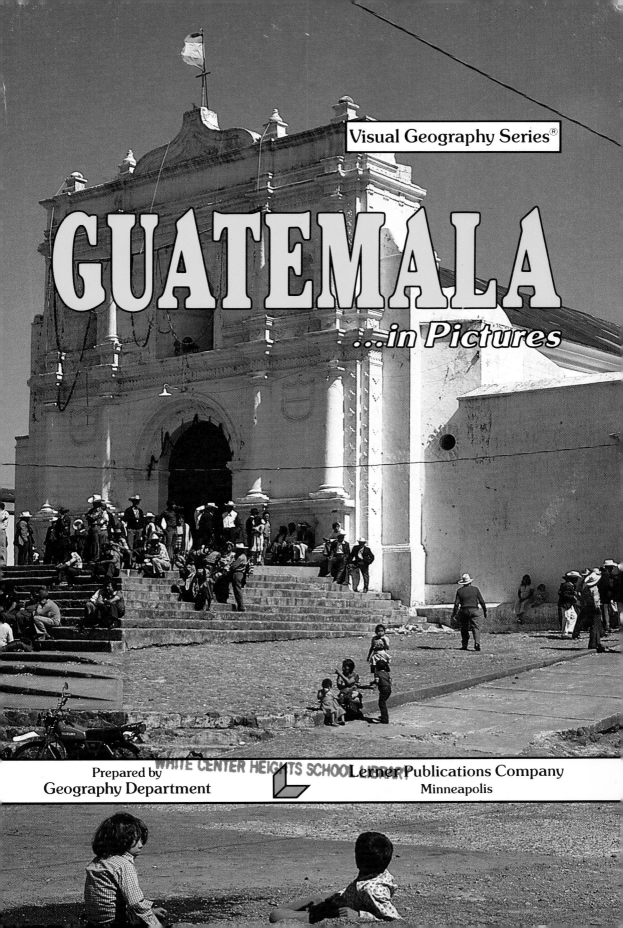

Visual Geography Series®

GUATEMALA
...in Pictures

Prepared by
Geography Department

Lerner Publications Company
Minneapolis

Courtesy of Pan-American Coffee Bureau

A Guatemalan worker handpicks the red cherries of a coffee tree.

This is an all-new edition of the Visual Geography Series. Previous editions have been published by Sterling Publishing Company, New York City, and some of the original textual information has been retained. New photographs, maps, charts, captions, and updated information have been added. The text has been entirely reset in 10/12 Century Textbook.

LIBRARY OF CONGRESS CATALOGING-IN-PUBLICATION DATA

Guatemala in pictures.

(Visual geography series)
Rev. ed. of: Guatemala in pictures / prepared by James Nach.
Includes index.
Summary: Describes the geography, history, economy, government, culture, and people of the northernmost Central American country.
1. Guatemala [1. Guatemala] I. Nach, James. Guatemala in pictures. II. Lerner Publications Company. Geography Dept. III. Series: Visual geography series (Minneapolis, Minn.)
F1463.G947 1987   972.81   86-15384
ISBN 0-8225-1803-1 (lib. bdg.)

International Standard Book Number: 0-8225-1803-1
Library of Congress Catalog Card Number: 86-15384

VISUAL GEOGRAPHY SERIES®

Publisher
Harry Jonas Lerner
Associate Publisher
Nancy M. Campbell
Executive Series Editor
Lawrence J. Zwier
Assistant Series Editor
Mary M. Rodgers
Editorial Assistant
Nora W. Kniskern
Illustrations Editor
Nathan A. Haverstock
Consultants/Contributors
Dr. Ruth F. Hale
Nathan A. Haverstock
Sandra K. Davis
Designer
Jim Simondet
Cartographer
Carol F. Barrett
Indexer
Kristine S. Schubert
Production Manager
Richard J. Hannah

Courtesy of Pan American Airways

Indians ready their canoes to cross Lake Atitlán.

Acknowledgments

Title page photo by Dr. Roma Hoff.

Elevation contours adapted from *The Times Atlas of the World*, seventh comprehensive edition (New York: Times Books, 1985).

3   4   5   6   7   8   9   10   96   95   94   93   92   91   90   89   88

Indian women fill their earthenware jugs with water at the village fountain in San Antonio, near Lake Atitlán.

Contents

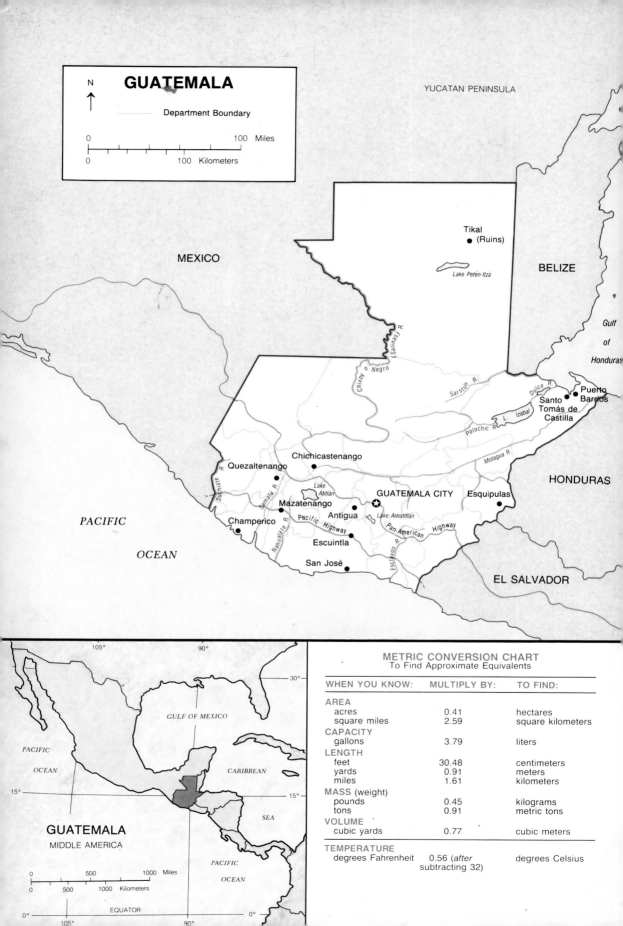

GUATEMALA

N

Department Boundary

0   100   Miles

0   100   Kilometers

YUCATAN PENINSULA

MEXICO

Tikal
● (Ruins)

Lake Petén-Itzá

BELIZE

Gulf

of

Honduras

(Salinas) R.

Chixoy o Negro R.

Sarstún R.

Dulce R.

Puerto
● Barrios

Santo
Tomás de
Castilla

L. Izabal

Polochic R.

Motagua R.

Chichicastenango

Quezaltenango

Samala R.

Suchiate R.

Lake Atitlán

GUATEMALA CITY
✪

Esquipulas
●

HONDURAS

Mazatenango

Nahualate R.

Pacific Highway

Antigua

Lake Amatitlán

Pan-American Highway

Champerico

PACIFIC

OCEAN

Escuintla

Esclavos R.

San José
●

EL SALVADOR

105°

90°

30°

GULF OF MEXICO

PACIFIC

OCEAN

CARIBBEAN

15°

15°

GUATEMALA

MIDDLE AMERICA

SEA

PACIFIC

OCEAN

0   500   1000   Miles

0   500   1000   Kilometers

EQUATOR

0°

0°

105°

90°

METRIC CONVERSION CHART
To Find Approximate Equivalents

WHEN YOU KNOW:	MULTIPLY BY:	TO FIND:
AREA		
acres	0.41	hectares
square miles	2.59	square kilometers
CAPACITY		
gallons	3.79	liters
LENGTH		
feet	30.48	centimeters
yards	0.91	meters
miles	1.61	kilometers
MASS (weight)		
pounds	0.45	kilograms
tons	0.91	metric tons
VOLUME		
cubic yards	0.77	cubic meters
TEMPERATURE		
degrees Fahrenheit	0.56 (*after* subtracting 32)	degrees Celsius

Schoolchildren march through the streets of Ciudad Vieja in preparation for Independence Day celebrations held on September 15. Public education and the celebration of national holidays are two of the forces leading Guatemala's Indians to participate more actively in national cultural affairs.

Introduction

More than any other Central American country, Guatemala is an Indian nation. *Mestizaje*, the mixing of European and Indian bloodlines, has occurred in Guatemala just as it has elsewhere in the region, but nearly half of Guatemala's population is still classified as Indian—meaning Indian in dress, language, cultural outlook, and way of life.

Guatemala is also a land where oligarchy (rule by a small elite group) has flourished. Guatemalans have had little to say about how they were governed by such groups—including the Spanish conquistadors and, before them, a priestly Indian caste. Representative government has not easily taken root in Guatemala. Assassinations, military coups, and revolutions have plagued the nation's leaders since its independence from Spain more than 150

years ago. In 1986, for the first time in 30 years, Guatemala inaugurated a popularly elected civilian as president—but he carries a loaded revolver at all times.

More than a thousand years ago, the sophisticated Mayan civilization flourished in Guatemala. Especially in the northern region known as the Petén, the remnants of large Mayan cities dominated by elaborate temples offer the twentieth century some hint of what was achieved by the ancestors of today's Guatemalan Indians. Modern Guatemala, however, has not been shaped so much by the Indians as by the descendants of the Spanish colonists. While Indian cultures have remained strong in Guatemala, they have stood apart from the European tradition that is the basis of Guatemala's legal and governmental structure. Even today, some

5

85 percent of Indian adults in Guatemala do not read or write Spanish—which has been the country's official language for nearly five centuries.

As Guatemala's economy and politics change, however, so do the lives of its Indians. Because of improved health care, there are more Indians. This means that there is too little land to parcel out to sons and daughters so that they, like their forebears, might go on raising corn and living in a secure culture where everything and everyone has a place. With little hope of inheriting land, the young move on—not so much drawn by the attractions of the outside world as pushed from behind by forces they do not comprehend. These young Indians take jobs in the mainstream of the Guatemalan economy, acquire material goods, and eventually find themselves estranged from the culture in which they were raised.

With increased participation in the Guatemalan economy, Indians are likely to be drawn more and more into the country's stormy political life. Some people claim that the Indians' apparent lack of interest in governmental affairs has allowed their culture to survive, that their separateness should be preserved to ensure the survival of their way of life. Practically speaking, the Indians of Guatemala now face choices, some of which involve them in the country's political struggles. They can choose to be part of the militias that the government puts together to suppress insurgencies, or they can join the insurgents. Their great numbers give them an awesome ability to effect the course Guatemala follows in the years to come.

With a conventional haircut and store-bought clothes, a young man has become a Ladino — an Indian who enters Guatemala's economic mainstream.

Lake Atitlán is 11 miles wide, 16 miles long, and in some places 1,500 feet deep. Volcanoes rise sharply from the edge of its strikingly blue waters.

1) The Land

Guatemala is the northernmost of the five Central American republics formed from the possessions of Spain during the nineteenth century. With a total area of 42,052 square miles, Guatemala is slightly smaller than the state of Tennessee. Within the country's borders lie landscapes ranging from moist tropical lowlands to cool mountains and plateaus. Four countries share boundaries with Guatemala. Mexico, with the longest frontier, lies to the west and north. Belize is to the east, and to the southeast, Honduras and El Salvador, two other Central American republics, fill out the balance of Guatemala's land boundary.

Guatemala has the advantage of fronting on two oceans. A 100-mile-long shoreline lies along the Gulf of Honduras, an arm of the Caribbean Sea. The country's most important ports, Santo Tomás de Castilla and Puerto Barrios, are both on this coast. Regular cargo-ship services connect them with New Orleans and other United States ports. The Pacific coast, while longer (151 miles), does not have the deep indentations found along the Caribbean (Atlantic) coast. San José and Champerico are Guatemala's leading ports on the Pacific.

Topography

The great chains of mountains that extend along the coasts of North and South America also pass through Central America. In Guatemala, the main range of mountains, the Sierra Madre, forms a sort of backbone running through the country parallel to the Pacific coast and about 50 miles inland. The nation's topography is divided into four regions: the Pacific coastal plain, the central highlands, the Atlantic littoral (a coastal region), and the Petén.

The Pacific coastal plain extends 160

Courtesy of Museum of Modern Art of Latin America

Located in the central highlands, at an elevation of more than 4,500 feet, Guatemala City enjoys a temperate climate throughout the year. The green hills and lofty mountains surrounding the city provide spectacular scenery.

miles from the Mexican border to El Salvador and has an average width of only 30 miles. Its soil, of volcanic origin, provides some of the best farmland in the nation. Inland from the coast yet west of the highlands is the Pacific Piedmont region, also known as the Boca Costa—an area of sugarcane plantations, rice farms, coffee plantations, and cattle ranches.

Rainfall at the town of Escuintla averages 96 inches a year, but other locations on the Pacific coast receive less precipitation. The area is amply watered, however, since 18 rivers flow through it. Because most are short and drop steeply from the Sierra Madre, they offer potential for hydroelectric development. Three are navigable, but only by small boats. The longest river on the Pacific side is the Suchiate, which has a length of 94 miles but is navigable for only 38. Other important rivers flowing to the Pacific are the Nahualate, the Samalá, and the Esclavos.

Photo by Dr. Roma Hoff

The route from Chimaltenango to Lake Atitlán, one the world's most scenic lakes, winds through rough mountain terrain.

Although the green quetzal bird is seen only in zoos and occasionally in the Petén forests, friendly parrots, such as these two large ones, are common.

Guatemala's second physical region, the central highlands, includes two almost parallel mountain chains—the Sierra Madre and the Altos Cuchumatanes. The latter range includes peaks 9,500 feet high in the western part of the country and extends northeast to the Atlantic Ocean. The Sierra Madre crosses the country from west to east, continuing into Honduras and El Salvador. On a central plateau between the two major mountain regions live most of Guatemala's people. Terraces, valleys, and the slopes of the Sierra Madre offer rich volcanic soils washed down during many centuries from the higher peaks. Guatemala City, Guatemala's capital and home to about one-fifth of its population, is situated on this plateau.

Two large lakes—Atitlán, which is 60 miles west of Guatemala City, and Amatitlán, 18 miles south of the capital—grace the central highlands. Atitlán, which is 16 miles long and 11 miles wide, is considered by many people, foreigners as well as Guatemalans, to be the most beautiful lake in the world. Three volcanoes and several Indian villages stand at its shores, and thermal springs feed mineral water into the lake.

Temperatures in Guatemala City, which is located at an elevation of 4,500 feet, average 64° F with little seasonal variation. Cool nights make blankets a necessity, while days are pleasantly warm. Precipitation occurs mostly between May and October, the cloudy, rainy season that residents of the area call winter.

Many of the highest mountains of the Sierra Madre are of volcanic origin. Most are inactive, but some are merely dormant and are likely to erupt at any time. Earthquakes are also frequent here, as in most Central American mountain areas. Both earthquakes and volcanic eruptions have caused great suffering to the inhabitants of the mountain highlands. Antigua, the old capital of Guatemala, was destroyed by the Agua Volcano in 1773. The Santa María Volcano brought ruin to Quezaltenango, the second largest city in the country, in 1902. A series of severe earthquakes in 1917 and 1918 destroyed much

A highway that slices through the jungle-covered plain leads to Flores, the capital of the Petén. The construction of roads and airstrips has helped to promote the development of this rich, but largely inaccessible, region.

of Guatemala City. An earthquake in central Guatemala in February 1976 killed more than 20,000 people and destroyed an estimated 200,000 dwellings.

Guatemala's volcanoes are the highest mountains in Central America. Tajumulco, whose summit reaches an elevation of 13,814 feet, is the tallest. Other well-known mountains are Tacaná (13,330 feet), located on the border with the Mexican state of Chiapas, and Atitlán (11,633 feet), which rises above the lake of the same name. In all, Guatemala has 34 important volcanoes within its borders.

The Atlantic littoral, Guatemala's third topographical area, is a region of lowlands. It contains the country's largest lake, Izabal, with an area of about 228 square miles, and large rivers such as the Motagua, Polochic, Dulce, and Sarstún. The Motagua, rising in the mountains near the famous Indian village of Chichicastenango, reaches the sea after 250 miles, its last 100 miles being navigable. Highway and railway connections from Guatemala City to the Atlantic coast parallel the course of the Motagua. For its last miles before reaching the sea, the Motagua forms the boundary between Guatemala and Honduras. Other important rivers emptying into the Caribbean are the Sarstún, forming the boundary with Belize, and the short Dulce, which drains into Lake Izabal. Steep, jungle-clad slopes rising above the Dulce—which is navigable for its entire 24-mile length—make this one of the most beautiful streams in Guatemala.

This Caribbean region, where some areas receive as much as 200 inches of rain annually, is the wettest part of the country. Both the mountains and the direction of the winds influence the amount of precipitation.

Jutting northward from central Guatemala is the great plain of Petén, the nation's fourth physical region. A limestone tableland with altitudes of no more than 650 feet, it has the same geological characteristics as the rest of the Yucatán Peninsula. Comprising about a third of Guatemala, the Petén is relatively unpopulated and covered mostly by jungles and some flat grasslands. It is dotted with lakes, ponds, and many water holes that form during the rainy season only to disappear into underground caverns during the dry season. Some of the most impressive Mayan ruins, including Tikal, lie slumbering in the jungles of the Petén.

Climate

Several factors effect temperature and precipitation patterns in Guatemala. First is its location within the tropics. Its northern border lies at a latitude only 18 degrees north of the equator, and its southernmost point is at only 14 degrees north latitude. Key West, Florida, the southernmost point in the continental United States, is at more than 24 degrees north latitude. On the average, tropical areas receive heat more steadily from the sun and therefore tend not to show the temperature variations that characterize higher latitudes.

Secondly, Guatemala is in the part of the

Guatemala's national flower is the white nun orchid, so named because of its resemblance to the silhouetted head of a nun. The *monja blanca,* as the flower is called in Spanish, grows wild only in the department of Alta Verapaz.

world directly affected by the trade winds. In the Northern Hemisphere, these winds blow steadily from the northeast. During the winter, they affect an area quite close to the equator, but during the summer

The Caves of Lanquin, in the department of Alta Verapaz, are ready-made for adventure inside the earth. Formed over the course of centuries by a fast-flowing underground river, these subterranean chambers have ceilings as high as 100 feet.

The residents of the capital city escape often to nearby Lake Amatitlán, even though swimming is unsafe because the water has become severely contaminated. The wealthy have vacation homes on its shores, and both rich and poor go to the lake for picnics, fishing, and boating.

Photo by Dr. Roma Hoff

The Agua and Fuego volcanoes tower over Antigua on one side, while a large cross dominates a hilltop on the other side of the city. Antigua was Guatemala's capital for 230 years before it was devastated by an earthquake in 1773. At its cultural height, Antigua was a center of religious art and higher learning, with 32 churches, 18 convents and monasteries, and 8 colleges within the city limits.

Courtesy of the Museum of Modern Art of Latin America

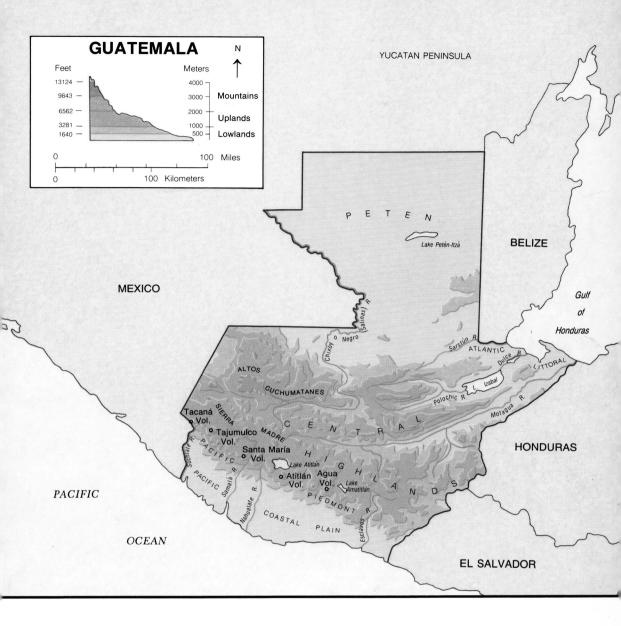

their coverage expands northward and includes Guatemala. From May through October, the trade winds bring moist air inland from the Gulf of Mexico. As this moist air is forced to rise over the mountains, it is cooled. Because the cooler air cannot retain such high amounts of moisture, condensation occurs and heavy rainfall results—especially in mountains facing the winds. Guatemala's east coast consequently receives more rain than its west coast, which is downwind from the mountains and is therefore in a rain shadow.

Another factor affecting climate, especially temperature, is elevation. Low-lying areas within the tropics tend to be warm, with temperatures ranging from 70° to 90° F. Only rarely does the mercury fall below 50° F in the *tierra caliente*, or hot country. Highland regions, on the other hand, are much more comfortable, with average temperatures of about 70° F

13

throughout the year. In Latin America, these regions of intermediate elevation and more moderate temperatures are called the *tierra templada*. At higher elevations, some mountain districts have average annual temperatures of 60° F or lower. During the cooler season of the year, November to March, freezing temperatures can occur in these higher places, which are consequently known as the *tierra fría*.

Flora and Fauna

Because of the great variety of climatic conditions within Guatemala's borders, many different types of vegetation thrive. There are palm trees in the lowlands, oaks and pines in the highlands, and hardy grasses clinging to the upper slopes of volcanoes. Among the most valuable of Guatemala's hundreds of types of trees is the mahogany of the jungle lowlands. Guatemala's national flower, the white nun orchid, flourishes in the forests of Alta Verapaz. Because of the cool climate in the highlands, many crops grown in countries of higher latitudes can also be grown in Guatemala. Among such crops are potatoes, maize (corn), and wheat.

Guatemala has little in the way of big game, but it does have a wide range of smaller wildlife. Among the larger animals are deer, wild pigs, armadillos, jaguars, bears, alligators, and several kinds of monkeys. The national bird is the beautiful quetzal. There are numerous species of insects, of which the mosquito, unfortunately, is the best known to man. (The mosquito problem decreases with altitude.)

Natural Resources

Economic development in much of Latin America historically has been delayed by a shortage of the kinds of energy—such as

Courtesy of Pan-American Coffee Bureau

The blossoms of a coffee tree are delicate and fragrant—they look and smell much like orange blossoms—but they are short-lived. After only a few days, the petals will fall away and small, round coffee cherries will begin to appear.

Jungle surrounds an oil exploration site in the Petén. Guatemala's industrial expansion depends heavily on the development of new domestic sources of energy. Oil wells are already operating in the department of Alta Verapaz, and hydroelectric facilities are harnessing the power of swift rivers flowing out of the mountains. If significant new oil deposits are discovered in the Petén, Guatemala will have to spend less to import foreign oil and will be able to channel its capital into domestic development.

Brushed by the mist of passing clouds, the smoking cone of Fuego Volcano rises above highland fields of corn and wheat. Despite the difficulty of cultivating such rolling terrain, the Indians who farm this area coax ample yields from the rich, volcanic soil. The pines that dot the fields and climb the steeper slopes are typical of Guatemala's highland forests. The cool temperatures at such altitudes encourage the growth of vegetation greatly different from the jungle plants that cover the Petén and other lowland areas.

coal, oil, and electricity—needed to fuel industry. Until the early 1980s, Guatemala was no exception to this rule. In 1980, however, it began drawing crude oil from wells in the Alta Verapaz department. The oil is being piped to Santo Tomás de Castilla, and further exploration is proceeding in the Petén. The nation has also begun to develop its hydroelectric potential, especially on the Pacific side of the Sierra Madre.

Mineral production includes zinc and lead concentrates, some antimony and tungsten, and small amounts of cadmium and silver. Copper is also being mined. Extraction of nickel ore in the northern part of the nation was begun in 1977 by the International Nickel Company of Canada, which was granted a 40-year concession to extract and process nickel ore. However, when a glut of nickel on the world market drove prices downward, production was suspended in the early 1980s.

Forests cover almost 18 million acres and provide valuable gums, oils, drugs, and dyes. The Petén is rich in mahogany and other woods, but tapping this resource is costly since the few rivers sufficiently large for rafting logs flow into either Mexico or Belize. Nonetheless, wood production in the early 1980s amounted to more than 36 million cubic feet. In 1983 Guatemala also exported fish worth about $9 million.

An especially well-paved section of the Pan-American Highway passes cornfields in the highlands of Guatemala near Citán. Except for a short gap in the wilderness near the Panama-Colombia border, this highway runs uninterrupted from Alaska to the southern tip of South America.

San Felipe Fort was built in the seventeenth century at the point where the Dulce River meets Lake Izabal. The purpose of this Spanish fort was to keep pirates from plundering lakeside warehouses where goods were stored for shipment to Spain.

2) History and Government

Long before Columbus landed in the New World, the Maya Indians—living in what is today Honduras, Guatemala, and southeastern Mexico—developed a civilization that in many ways was the equal of ancient Egypt's. While most Indians in the Western Hemisphere remained primitive hunters and gatherers until forced off their lands by the white man, the Maya were able to create a great culture.

The Maya

The time when the Maya first arrived in the Petén is not known, but it was probably before 1000 B.C. At first, they merely cleared away the jungle and planted their crops. Later, because they needed to know when growing seasons for crops would begin, they turned to astronomy to find out the length of the year. In order to make celestial measurements and calculations and to measure distances on earth, the Maya developed a number system that included the concept of zero, a concept that neither the ancient Greeks nor the ancient Romans employed. Mayan astronomers calculated the length of the year more accurately than did those who formulated the Julian calendar—which was used in England and its colonies until the mid-eighteenth century.

Like the Egyptians, the Maya developed a system of hieroglyphic writing. Unfortunately, archaeologists are unable to interpret much of what the Maya wrote (and there is little chance of discovering an equivalent of the Rosetta stone in Central America). The Maya were also great architects and designers. Working only with stone tools, they proved to be superb carvers, potters, and builders. They worshipped many different gods—most of whom were connected with the seasons and stars.

Mayan cities, such as Tikal in the Petén of northern Guatemala, were large even by today's standards. Archaeologists believe that the larger cities had populations ranging from 100,000 to 400,000. There was no unified Mayan empire. Instead, the different Mayan settlements were run in somewhat the same way as the Greek city-states (Athens and Sparta, for example). In the central portions of cities were temples and various religious and administrative buildings. Most of the people lived in thatched huts around the central core of each city and farmed the fields beyond the populated areas. The people were divided into four classes: the hereditary rulers, the nobility and priesthood, the farmers and craftspersons, and the slaves. Power rested in the hands of the nobles and priests; the great temples were the sites of elaborate religious rites performed by the priests.

The high point of Mayan civilization in Guatemala was reached between the fourth and seventh centuries. Then, for reasons not entirely known today, the Maya abandoned their cities in Guatemala and migrated northward to the Yucatán Peninsula, where they built Chichén Itzá,

Photo by Dr. Roma Hoff

The greatest of the Mayan ruins is Tikal, in Guatemala's Petén. The site of this huge city was discovered in 1848—after having lain abandoned for more than 1,000 years—and was made a national park in 1956. The ancient city, which was once home to 400,000 people, covers nine square miles. At the right are two pyramidic temples facing one another across a large plaza. Visitors to Tikal can climb one of these temples by hanging onto a huge chain while walking up the side of the pyramid.

The stone steps on which these Indians rest, socialize, and sell their produce now lead to a Catholic church, but they once led to a Mayan pyramid.

Uxmal, and other splendid cities. Various reasons have been put forward to explain why the Maya left settlements in Guatemala's Petén. Some authorities believe disease or natural disaster was responsible for the migration. Others maintain that the Maya left because they had exhausted the soil and forests of the region.

One group of Maya returned to the Petén in about the twelfth century and established a city on an island in Lake Petén-Itzá. Discovered accidentally by the Spanish in 1697, this last independent Mayan settlement was soon overrun by the Europeans, and its inhabitants were scattered.

Spanish Conquest

In 1517, a Spanish expedition led by Francisco Fernández de Córdoba sailed westward from Cuba and reached the coast of Yucatán. The Spaniards were driven off by hostile Maya Indians, and Fernández was mortally wounded in the fighting. Two years later, Hernando Cortés, his appetite whetted by tales of the riches of Mexico, set sail without the permission of the jealous governor of Cuba. With him went a force of 553 Spanish soldiers and 16 horses. By August 1521, Cortés had subdued the great Aztec Empire and become ruler of Mexico.

One of Cortés's bravest lieutenants was Pedro de Alvarado, who had distinguished himself in the battles with the Aztecs. In 1523, he and his army of 420 Spanish soldiers left Mexico for Guatemala. The goal of the Spanish conquistadors was to gain power—by diplomacy or war—over the Indian kingdoms and their presumed riches. At first the Indians believed the

Like many of the other bowls found at Tikal, this skillfully painted stucco bowl has a bird-shaped handle at the top. This design feature may indicate that such bowls were imported from Mexico or made at Tikal by Mexican artisans.

The Great Temple of the Giant Jaguar at Tikal is one of the major attractions at this ancient Mayan city. Visitors to the site clamber up the steep steps of the temple, where Mayan priests performed religious rites a thousand years ago. Other visitors inspect the elaborately sculpted stelae—stone pillars—found there. Tikal could become Guatemala's greatest tourist attraction.

The doorways of Mayan temples were often surmounted by carved wooden lintels that lent support to the structure and added to the beauty of the passageway.

The Palace of the Captains General at Antigua was completed in 1764, just in time to be wrecked in the earthquake of 1773. Meant to be the finest building in the captaincy general when it was built, it has now been restored and houses the administrative offices of the department of Sacatepéquez.

bearded white men on horseback to be gods, but the Spaniards' thirst for money and glory soon cured the Indians of this notion.

Alvarado's advance into Guatemala was opposed at every turn by Tecum Umán, who led the Quichés—an important tribe of Indians living in the highlands. After defeating the Indians in several preliminary battles, the Spaniards advanced on the plains where the city of Quezaltenango now stands. There the battle was joined with a large army led personally by Tecum Umán, who, at the height of the fighting, challenged Alvarado to personal combat. The Indian leader killed Alvarado's horse but was slain by the Spaniard. After Tecum Umán's death, the conquistadors routed the Indian army, and other Indian tribes soon submitted peacefully to Spanish rule or were destroyed in battle.

The first Spanish capital of Guatemala was founded in July 1524 and named Santiago de los Caballeros. Soon, new troubles arose with the Indians. At the time of the Spanish conquests, there was no colonial office in the mother country to administer the new possessions. Instead, Cortés, Alvarado, and other Spanish leaders ruled as they saw fit. They also devoted much time to intriguing against one another. A revolt in Guatemala was caused during Alvarado's absence by his brother's tyrannical rule. Alvarado, upon returning, crushed the revolt.

Because of clashes with the Indians, the capital was moved in 1527 to what is now known as Ciudad Vieja. Fourteen years later, Alvarado died in Mexico while leading a charge against hostile Indians. His widow, a forceful woman, had herself proclaimed governess of Guatemala—but her

21

term in office was short and marked by disaster. There had been thunderstorms for several days, and on the day she assumed power (September 10, 1541) a flood of water and mud released by an earthquake destroyed the city and killed most of the inhabitants, including Alvarado's widow.

A new capital (today called Antigua) was built after this great disaster, and it served as the seat of Spanish government until 1773—when it too was destroyed by a series of catastrophic earthquakes.

Colonial Life

By 1568, Antigua had been firmly established as the capital of the captaincy general of Guatemala, which consisted of present-day Guatemala, Chiapas (now part of Mexico), Honduras, El Salvador, Nicaragua, and Costa Rica. Each of the provinces was ruled by a governor who was subordinate—at least in theory—to the captain general at Antigua. Activities of the captain general and other officials were controlled by a body known as the Real (Royal) Audiencia, which reported back directly to the king of Spain.

Spanish colonial rule was strict and uncompromising. Unlike the English colonies in North America, which were self-governing to a large degree, Spanish settlements in the Americas received all their orders from Spain. Administrative posts in the captaincy general of Guatemala were sold to Spanish noblemen who were friends of the king. Creoles—as Spaniards born in the New World were called—were not permitted to be part of the higher circles of

The abandoned cloister at Santa Clara near Antigua has been so severely damaged by earthquake activity that entrance to the interior is prohibited. Walking in the vicinity is strictly restricted to the outer perimeters of the ruins.

The National Palace, on the main square in Guatemala City, is of Spanish colonial design. The second floor features intricate wrought-iron railings.

colonial government. In addition, the Indian population was oppressed and enslaved.

The Spanish hoped to convert the Indians to Roman Catholicism. In this ambition the conquerors were largely disappointed, for the Indians had no desire to give up their old gods. However, the Catholic orders—the Franciscans, Dominicans, Jesuits, and others—worked hard and built hundreds of churches, monasteries, and convents throughout the captaincy general of Guatemala. To reward the orders for their activities, the Spanish government granted them large parcels of land and slaves to work the fields. Most of the orders soon became rich and powerful. Some clergymen, however, such as Fray Bartolomé de las Casas and Bishop

Francisco Marroquín, worked hard to try to better the lot of the Indians.

Spain treated its colonies in the New World only as sources of wealth for the mother country. European animals and crops—such as sheep, cattle, and wheat—were brought over from Spain. At the same time, local production of certain products (wine and olives, among others) was outlawed to prevent competition with Spain's own industries. Exports of tobacco, indigo, cotton, sarsaparilla, quinine, cacao, and other desired Guatemalan products were encouraged. Heavy taxes were levied on exports and imports, especially since Guatemala did not produce as much gold and silver as the Spanish government had hoped it would.

Many of the regulations of the Spanish

23

Working in their spare time on weeknights and weekends, people of a suburb of Antigua make bricks that they will use in building their own homes. The new homes constructed under this government-sponsored program will be of Spanish colonial design, in keeping with the traditional architecture of the old city.

government were unrealistic. Smuggling and corruption in Guatemala were natural consequences of poor judgment on the part of the Spanish imperial government. An added danger to trade came from foreign adventurers and pirates. They ranged from flamboyant corsairs—such as Sir Francis Drake, who preyed on Spanish shipping with the unofficial consent of England's Queen Elizabeth I—to less glamorous pirates who terrorized the Caribbean well into the eighteenth century.

Although life was not pleasant for the Indians and the lower social classes under colonial rule, the Spanish nobles and (to a lesser extent) the Creoles lived lives of great comfort once the pioneer days of life in the New World were past. Spanish artisans and craftspersons also reaped some of the riches of life in the captaincy general of Guatemala. Wealthier Spaniards living there transplanted the architecture and culture of their homeland to the New World. Their houses, built to resemble those they had left in Spain, were constructed with thick outside walls, grille-covered windows, and thick wooden doors usually studded with brass. Inside the

24

main entrance was the patio, around which the rooms of the house were built. The homes of the rich were virtual private museums containing the finest work of artists and craftspersons in Guatemala and Spain.

Lavish celebrations were held on public holidays. Bullfights and tournaments took place, and men and women of noble birth wore their most elaborate costumes bedecked with jewels, gold, and silver. The fiestas usually lasted several days and included fireworks displays and music that blended Spanish and Indian rhythms.

The End of Spanish Rule

During the sixteenth century, Spain was Europe's greatest colonial power. The gold, silver, and agricultural products taken

Independent Picture Service

Throughout Antigua, ruins recall the architectural glories of Guatemala's colonial past.

Independent Picture Service

Many Indian villages in the highlands have changed little since the colonial era. The large church seen here is still as well kept as it was in the time of the Spanish. Women still fill their water jars at the fountains located in village squares. The steel pipes at this old fountain, however, are a twentieth-century innovation.

25

This arch is all that remains standing of a church and convent at Antigua. Earthquakes in 1717 and 1751 leveled the buildings that housed one of the early religious orders in Guatemala.

from the Spanish colonies made Spain one of the wealthiest countries in the world. Unfortunately, Spain's glory soon waned. Powerful rivals arose in northern Europe to challenge the overseas supremacy of the Spanish. The great Spanish attempt to crush Protestant England ended with the loss of the Spanish fleet, the Armada, in 1588.

Poor colonial government was mainly responsible for the decay of Spain's empire. In Guatemala and other Spanish possessions, the Indians and the lower classes were kept in poverty and ignorance. The Creoles, who were discriminated against only because they were colonial-born, eventually proved to be the most independent and strong-willed people enduring Spanish misrule. Because many of them were educated and prosper-

ous, Creoles were able to gain knowledge of events occurring beyond the borders of Guatemala and to come into contact with writings about liberty and freedom.

Two foreign events encouraged the desire for independence among Guatemala's Creoles. These were the successful revolt of Britain's North American colonies in 1776 and the French Revolution in 1789. The Jesuits, whom Spain had expelled from its overseas possessions in 1767, also desired an end to Spanish rule.

At the beginning of the nineteenth century, the Bourbon monarchy in Spain was temporarily overthrown by Napoleon. Soon, the flame of revolt spread throughout Spanish possessions in the New World. Several anti-Spanish conspiracies were uncovered in Guatemala during the first two decades of the nineteenth century. By

1821, with Spanish power crumbling to the north and south, it was obvious to all but the staunchest royalists that the days of Spanish rule were numbered.

Gabino Gaínza, the acting captain general, called a meeting of the heads of all factions on September 15, 1821. An Act of Independence was drawn up and signed after Gaínza and the other royalists realized that opposition was hopeless. Gaínza did not merely sign the Act of Independence —he had himself made president. Thus the last captain general of colonial Guatemala became the first ruler of independent Guatemala.

Independence

The colonies that had gained their independence in 1821 were poorly prepared for self-government. Central America soon found itself overrun by the army of Agustín de Iturbide, who had had himself proclaimed emperor of Mexico. In 1822, however, Iturbide was overthrown, and his empire fell to pieces. Representatives of the states of the former captaincy general of Guatemala met in 1823 and 1824 and drew up a constitution for the Federation of Central America—styling the document after the United States Constitution.

Turmoil—rather than progress—was the keynote of the federation. The first president, Manuel José Arce of El Salvador, was extremely conservative and was soon overthrown by the Liberals headed by General Francisco Morazán of Honduras. Morazán introduced many reforms and curbed the power of the Roman Catholic Church. The Conservatives under Rafael Carrera, however, overthrew the Liberal government in Guatemala in 1838, and the

Drummers and buglers lead schoolgirls in a practice march for an Independence Day parade. When Guatemala and the rest of Central America declared themselves independent on September 15, 1821, Spain was too weak to challenge them.

Francisco Morazán, a Honduran, was the last president of the ill-fated Federation of Central America, of which Guatemala was a member. For all practical purposes, the federation had disintegrated by 1839, but Guatemala did not officially leave it until 1847.

Dr. Mariano Gálvez was elected Guatemala's head of state in 1831, during the days when it was a member of the Federation of Central America. A member of Francisco Morazán's Liberal Party, he was responsible for instituting many important social reforms.

federation disintegrated. (Guatemala officially left the federation in 1847, long after the other Central American states had left it.) From 1839 to 1865, Carrera was the most powerful man in Guatemala, although he sometimes retired temporarily from the political scene. Liberals from the other Central American republics tried to overthrow the reactionary Conservative regime in Guatemala in 1851 but were defeated in battle by Carrera, who then became president for life. He died in 1865 and was succeeded by Vicente Cerna, who continued his predecessor's wasteful policies.

In 1867, the first of several Liberal revolts against the tyranny of Cerna broke out. Cerna crushed the first challenges to

Independent Picture Service

Disparities between the living conditions of the rich and of the poor have long been a source of strain on Guatemalan society. The slums of a modern-day village testify that the longstanding battle to provide clean and safe housing to Guatemala's poor is far from won.

Independent Picture Service

Two Indians in gaily colored traditional costume perform an ancient Mayan dance. In the background, several musicians play the popular marimba, an instrument introduced to Latin America by African slaves. The keys of the marimba are made from selected Guatemalan woods.

Independent Picture Service

Before any excavation is performed at Tikal and other Mayan sites, careful surveys are conducted. Excavation at Tikal began in 1956, and in 1965 the Guatemalan government committed funds for the restoration and preservation of the ruined city.

his rule, and the leaders either fled to Mexico or were killed by government troops. In 1871, however, Justo Rufino Barrios and Miguel García Granados—Liberals exiled in Mexico—invaded Guatemala. Thousands flocked to their standard, and the Cerna dictatorship ended.

Social Reform Begins

During the Liberal regimes of García Granados and Barrios, progress toward social reform was made in education, finance, administration, and the granting of freedom of religion. Barrios ordered roads and railways built and encouraged foreign trade. His severe measures restricting the activities of the Catholic Church were patterned after those of his friend Benito Juárez, president of Mexico. Unfortunately, Barrios dreamed of another Central American federation, and he tried to impose his wish on the other republics by force. He was killed during the battle of Chalchuapa in El Salvador in 1885.

After the death of Barrios, Guatemala experienced several decades of varied governments. José María Reyna Barrios, president from 1892 until his assassination in 1898, ruled with good intentions and even organized the first Central American Exposition, held in 1897. However, he had a weakness for printing paper money to pay for the costs of government, and this method of finance proved harmful to commerce. Manuel Estrada Cabrera, who be-

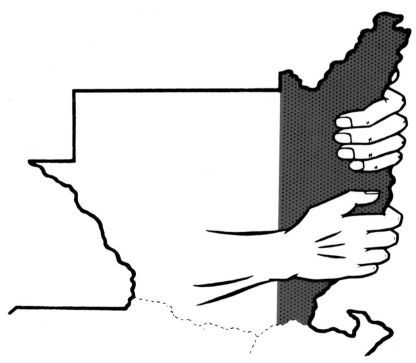

A Guatemalan political cartoon depicts hands stretching from Guatemala to grasp Belize (formerly British Honduras). Even though Belize is now an independent country, Guatemala still claims it and maps published in Guatemala customarily show the area as a Guatemalan province. The Guatemalan claim to Belize arises from Britain's failure to abide by a nineteenth century agreement: Britain was to have built a road through the Petén to Guatemala City in exchange for control over Belize. The road was never built, and Guatemala claimed—but never exercised—the right to retake the disputed territory.

The fluted columns of the cathedral in Guatemala City bear the marks of a 1970 earthquake. Guatemala's history is one of continual adaptation to the ravages of earthquakes. Deep beneath Guatemala, one of the great plates that make up the earth's crust—the Cocos Plate—is moving northeast and forcing itself under another plate, the larger and more stable American Plate. Sometimes an irregularity in one of the plates snags the other, and tremendous strain builds up at the point of the snag. Eventually, the strain will be too great, the snag will break, and almost incomprehensible forces will be transmitted to the surface in the form of shock waves. As these waves shake the surface, buildings sway and crack, bridges twist, and people are in great danger of being struck by falling objects.

Courtesy of Museum of Modern Art of Latin America

came president in 1898, managed to head off financial disaster, but he also chose to keep himself in power by using dictatorial methods. Cabrera ruthlessly destroyed any opposition to his rule for over two decades. In 1920, a revolution broke out, overthrowing the Cabrera regime.

Modern Times

During the period from 1920 to 1930, Guatemala had six successive heads of state. General Jorge Ubico, who was elected president in 1930, ruled for 14 years—using the armed forces to maintain power. However, the Ubico regime had many accomplishments to its credit. Government finances were put in order, internal communications and transport were improved, foreign trade was expanded, and numerous public buildings were constructed.

Ubico's dictatorship was overthrown by a popular revolt on June 30, 1944. After another army general failed in an attempted coup d'état, a new constitution was drawn up for the nation and, in elections held in 1945, Dr. Juan José Arévalo was elected president. Arévalo, a socialist, instituted far-reaching social reforms during his term of office. The reforms were aimed at giving workers more rights, bringing the large Indian population into the mainstream of Guatemalan life, and cracking down on the small number of domestic and foreign firms that controlled much of the nation's economy. Unfortunately, laws were also passed to curtail the activities of the political opposition to the Arévalo government.

In 1951, Colonel Jacobo Arbenz Guzmán took office as Arévalo's elected successor. Arbenz tried to introduce agrarian reform, and in 18 months a great amount of uncultivated land owned by the wealthy—about 1.5 million acres—was taken over by the government and given to some 100,000 families. Opposition to such reform, however, came from the United Fruit Company, which held enormous amounts of land (85 percent of it unused), and from the United States government, then fearful of Communist influences in Latin America. In 1954 this led to intervention directed by the Central Intelligence Agency. Arbenz fled and was succeeded by Colonel Carlos Castillo Armas, who undid many of the social reforms of the previous decade. Land that had been given to peasants was returned to landlords, the power of trade unions was broken, and illiterate people were denied the vote—which in Guatemala meant that 7 out of 10 persons were disenfranchised. Castillo Armas was assassinated in 1957 by a member of his own entourage.

In the wake of Castillo Armas's undoing of a decade of reform, the nature of Guatemalan politics changed. Instead of the familiar squabbling among factions of the oligarchy, a struggle arose between the right and the left. The right continued to represent the traditional ruling interests, while the left attracted newly prominent professionals and military officers, who were willing to stir up discontent to get ahead or create a more just society. Assassination became commonplace in the ongoing political feud.

Political divisions in Guatemala were sometimes deepened by U.S. support for authoritarian leaders. These leaders served

A cut stem of bananas is carried out of a plantation near the town of Bananera. Banana-producing companies based in the United States have long owned much of Guatemala's productive land and have exercised great political influence in Guatemala. The United States government has often supported authoritarian rulers in Guatemala who protected the interests of these U.S. companies but who showed little interest in the demands of Guatemalans for a more equitable distribution of land.

Cakchiquel Indians, wearing homemade shirts of their village's intricate, distinctive design, trade at the open-air market of Patzún. The Cakchiquels have recently been the targets of military attack by the government, which is trying to stop alleged revolutionary activity among the Indians.

U.S. interests by opposing Communism and allowing foreign businesses to operate in Guatemala with few restrictions; they also sternly supressed dissent. One such leader was President Miguel Ydígoras Fuentes (in office from 1958 to 1963). He secretly allowed the U.S. Central Intelligence Agency to use Guatemalan territory for training the Cuban exiles who conducted the ill-fated Bay of Pigs invasion of Cuba in 1961. When this became known, angry Guatemalan nationalists joined forces with the leftists—who advocated a Cuba-style revolution in Guatemala—and overthrew Ydígoras.

Young officers of the Guatemalan military, including leftist-nationalists Marco Antonio Yon Sosa and Luis Augusto Turcios Lima, organized a guerrilla movement after becoming embittered by what they saw as submissiveness to the United States among their superiors. During the late 1960s, the insurrection heated up, and three prominent U.S. officials—the ambassador, the director of the embassy's military mission, and a naval attaché—were assassinated.

In response, Guatemala's rulers organized right-wing death squads—civilian vigilante groups who, working sometimes with military forces and sometimes independently, murdered suspected guerrillas, guerrilla sympathizers, and others who fit their rather broad definition of "Communists." In a particularly brutal campaign to wipe out insurgency in Zacapa department (northeast of Guatemala City), more than 2,000 people were killed in a six-month period ending in May 1971. The leaders of this campaign provided

33

Guatemala's top leadership over the next decade, a violent time in which Guatemala's military supressed any hint of political activism by such groups as trade unions, rural cooperatives, and university students.

Military coups were frequent in the early 1980s, but eventually Guatemala's military, bowing to international pressure, saw fit to hold elections. On January 14, 1986, Marco Vinicio Cerezo Arévalo, of the center-left Christian Democratic Party, was sworn in as Guatemala's first popularly elected civilian president in more than 30 years. Cerezo Arévalo may represent a step away from the violence that has long characterized Guatemalan politics, but—conscious of recent history—he always carries a loaded revolver and is accompanied by heavily armed bodyguards.

Guatemala Accord

In February 1987 Costa Rican president Oscar Arias Sánchez put forth a Central American peace proposal. Arias's plan—since referred to as the Guatemala Accord—called for scheduled cease-fires, free elections, committees to solve local disagreements, and other democratic reforms. On August 7, 1987, the chief executives of Honduras, El Salvador, Nicaragua, Guatemala, and Costa Rica met to sign the accord.

Supporters of the plan are hopeful that its 90-day adjustment period will produce lasting peace in the region. Critics point to the timing of the plan, calling it a means to force foreign countries—including the United States and Cuba—to cut off their aid to Central American rebels. Other critics argue that the governments involved have no intention of meeting rebel leaders at the polling booths.

Nevertheless, if carried through as written, the accord would end civil wars in Nicaragua, El Salvador, and Guatemala. Furthermore, the plan would evict rebels, who are fighting guerrilla wars against those three governments, from Honduran and Costa Rican soil. Such a return of each rebel group to its own country would con-

A young Indian boy helps his father in their cornfield in the Quiché region. Since this boy is the first-born child in the family, he stands a good chance of inheriting the family land and being able to pursue the traditional life of a highland farmer. His younger brothers and sisters, however, may not be so lucky. Indian lands have been subdivided among children so often that there is no longer enough to go around. More and more Indian children are being forced to leave their ancestral lands and seek jobs in the cities. One of the goals of land-reform advocates in Guatemala is to reduce this problem by granting Indians ownership of land that is potentially productive but is held unused by large corporations and a few very wealthy families.

Courtesy of United Nations

Industrial experts from many nations—including Austria, India, Paraguay, and Costa Rica—meet around a conference table in Guatemala City. The conferees, whose discussion has been sponsored by the United Nations, are voicing their opinions on industrial development in Central America.

siderably ease international tensions in the region.

Judiciary and Local Government

The judicial system in Guatemala is similar to those in other Western countries. At the lowest level are the Peace Courts. Above these are the Courts of First Instance, the Court of Appeals, and the Supreme Court.

For administrative purposes, Guatemala is divided into 22 departments (provinces). Each of the departments is administered by a governor who is appointed by the head of state. The departments are not semi-independent units as are the U.S. states; they simply bring the power of the central government closer to the people.

More often than not, governors do not even come from the department to which they are appointed, but merely carry out the policy of the national government in Guatemala City.

The departments vary greatly in size and population. For example, the governor of the Petén is responsible for 13,843 square miles but only about 102,000 people; the governor of the department of Guatemala, which includes Guatemala City, has 1.7 million people in his 821-square-mile department.

Local government is carried out by councils called *municipios*. Largely independent of the central government, municipios are composed of officials elected by the local residents. Each municipio governs several villages, its size depending on the density of the local population.

Foreign Relations

Guatemala has traditionally sought to secure control over the adjacent Crown Colony of British Honduras, now independent and known as Belize. In the days when buccaneers roamed the Caribbean, one of their number, a Scotsman named Wallis or Wallace, settled with some woodcutters on a small island off the coast of present-day Belize, beat off Spanish attacks, and claimed the surrounding territory for Britain. Later, other British settlers arrived from Jamaica, attracted by the valuable timber in the gulf area. In 1859, the Republic of Guatemala recognized the British claim on the condition that the British government build a road through the jungles of the Petén to Guatemala City.

The highway was never built, and Guatemala claimed in 1938 that British Honduras belonged to Guatemala by default. Even today, all Guatemalan maps show Belize as part of the national territory of Guatemala and call it Belice (possibly a corruption of the pirate Wallace's name).

The Republic of Guatemala is a charter member of the United Nations and is a member of the Organization of American States (OAS).

Courtesy of Museum of Modern Art of Latin America

The white columns and graceful arches of the Civic Center of Guatemala, a governmental building, are among the features that contribute to the attractiveness of this urban plaza. In the cities, as in most villages, plazas around which important buildings cluster become popular gathering places and centers of civic activity.

Photo by Dr. Roma Hoff

The church of Santo Tomás in Chichicastenango is famous for the "folkcatholicism" that the Indians practice. The Indians who ritually burn corn and alcohol on the church steps in the morning will probably attend a Catholic Mass later in the day.

3) The People

Guatemala, the most populous country in Central America, had an estimated 8.9 million inhabitants in 1987. Because of Guatemala's small size and relatively large population, its population density exceeds those of all but four countries in the Western Hemisphere (Haiti, El Salvador, Cuba, and the Dominican Republic). This population density of slightly more than 200 persons per square mile is, however, far below the United Kingdom's 600 inhabitants per square mile.

The distribution of the Guatemalan people is very uneven. The highland areas, because they have the most comfortable climate, are the most heavily populated. The Petén, which includes much of Guatemala's jungle lowlands, is practically uninhabited—the population density is only about seven persons per square mile. Other lowland areas along the Caribbean and Pacific are also sparsely inhabited when compared to the highlands.

Guatemala City, with a metropolitan population of approximately 1.3 million, is the only large city in the country. The second largest city, Quezaltenango, has about 66,000 residents. Other towns are Puerto

37

Mazatenango, and Antigua, the old Spanish capital that was destroyed by earthquakes in 1773 and rebuilt.

The people of Guatemala have traditionally been spoken of as belonging to one of two groups—Ladinos or Indians. According to this classification, anyone (regardless of ethnic background) who adopted a Western way of life was a Ladino and anyone who adhered to the traditional Indian way of life was an Indian. It is more common now, however, to reserve the term *Ladino* for those of Indian blood who have taken on Western ways.

Young Indians who have little hope of inheriting land on which to raise crops often become Ladinos out of economic necessity. It is a transformation that can alienate the Ladino forever from the people among whom he or she has grown up. The Indians who stay in the village may look on the Ladino as a kind of defector to an alien life—store-bought clothes, a job among strangers, the accumulation of material possessions. The Ladino may come to associate the old ways with a sort of passive willingness to be exploited by Hispanic outsiders. Many Ladinos truly cannot go home again.

Slightly fewer than half of all Guatemalans are of pure Indian stock. Other important ethnic groups in Guatemala include the mestizos—people of mixed Spanish and Indian descent—and people of pure Spanish blood. Guatemala's population also includes a small number of people of German, English, Chinese, and U.S. origin. As might be expected, rural areas are populated mainly by Indians. Tensions have arisen between the mestizos and the Indians as the Indians have begun to demand a stronger voice in the decision-making process.

Courtesy of Inter-American Development Bank

A young woman fills water jugs at a public fountain in the village of Santa María de Jesús. She wears traditional dress, but she has made a concession to modernity—the lightweight plastic jugs she uses instead of much heavier traditional clay containers.

38

These girls of the Caribbean lowlands have features that reflect the racial mixing—of Indian, white, and black—common among the people of this region.

Family incomes vary greatly, with those in the cities much higher than those in the rest of the country. The average per capita income in cities is equivalent to about $325 per month, while in rural areas the average income is closer to the equivalent of $60 per month. Large numbers of city-dwellers own cars, television sets, and other conveniences. Some—but not many—families in small towns also have these items.

It is estimated that about 12 percent of the people in the nation live in absolute poverty. Only 11 percent have safe water piped into their homes, and only 22 percent have electricity. (In the United States, these basic utilities reach 98 percent and 99 percent of the population, respectively.)

Life expectancy in Guatemala is low, even for Central America, but the population growth rate remains high—3.2 percent per year.

The father usually supports the family, but sometimes the mother must work. Children, especially of the poor, often work as soon as they are able. In rural areas, small family industries—often producing textiles—are common.

Black beans are basic to the diet of most Guatemalans and are as popular in Guatemala as hamburgers are in the United States. Other main foods include some meat, rice, other vegetables, and tortillas. Also popular are tamales, cornmeal or rice dough filled with meat and spices; fried yucca, a starch plant; and fried plátano, a banana-like fruit, eaten with honey and cream. Obtaining well-balanced meals can be difficult, particularly for rural Guatemalans. In larger cities, especially in the capital, eating habits are cosmopolitan.

Courtesy of David Mangurian

The Indians

Guatemala's Indians lead a life rather different from that of Westernized Guatemalans. Although the Indians have been greatly affected by their contact with European civilization since the time of the conquest, they have retained much of their traditional culture. In parts of the highlands, Indian tongues—not Spanish—are the primary languages of the inhabitants. In urban areas and in the lowlands, Spanish is the most widely spoken language. Most Guatemalans are members of the Roman Catholic faith, but the Indians still adhere to many practices of their traditional worship.

Most Indians live in villages dating from after the Spanish conquest. In villages, the Spaniards hoped, the Indians could be protected more easily from unscrupulous Europeans and could be brought under the influence of Catholicism. To attract In-

39

Residents of a highland village set their clothes out to dry in the noonday sun. The clear air and the strong tropical sunshine quickly dry the array of colorful garments.

dians to villages, Spanish priests planted corn, erected huts, and began work on churches. Indians soon moved into the huts and harvested the corn at the invitation of priests.

In a typical Guatemalan village, the church is the most prominent landmark. Facing the church is the village square containing a well and trees. Government buildings and privately owned shops border the other sides of the square. Homes are constructed of adobe (sun-dried brick) or stone, with roofs of tile or thatch.

A homemade altar, on which a figure of the baby Jesus rests below a picture of St. Joseph and the Christ Child, is decorated with calla lilies and hanging fruit. Visitors are rarely allowed to see, let alone photograph, the altars that many Guatemalan Indians keep in their homes.

40

The Maya were known throughout Central America and Mexico as excellent artisans. Keeping alive a craft practiced by his ancestors, an elderly Indian rhythmically operates a spinning wheel to make twine.

In lowland areas, houses are built on stilts because of the moist, hot climate. A village home almost always has a small altar displaying a picture of the family's patron saint and adorned with offerings and incense burners. Most Indian homes, whether in the highlands or the lowlands, consist of one or two neatly kept rooms. Furniture is usually sparse, and Indians often sleep on mats rather than on beds.

Life is not easy for Guatemalan Indians, and sickness and death are always present in most villages. However, Indians have learned to take these things in stride. Death is not thought to be a great tragedy, for the departed one is believed to be beginning a happier life in the next world. In fact, villagers often hold great feasts with accompanying fireworks displays

Outside the brightly painted houses of a highland village, men, women, and children begin gathering early on a market day. Those who live far outside the village rise well before dawn to make the trip to market on foot or by mule.

These Indian women, whose features mark them as descended from the Maya, learned early in life how to carry loads by balancing baskets, jugs, and other containers on their heads.

when an important person dies. In many parts of the country, Indians bury their dead with various household articles for use in the next world. On All Saints' Day in November, yellow flowers are displayed in homes and placed on graves. Village church bells toll throughout the day in memory of the dead.

Birth and marriage are also recognized as important milestones in Indian life. Ceremonies vary from place to place in the country, but they frequently include both native and Christian rituals. Children are baptized as soon as possible after birth, because both the Christian religion and Indian custom hold that such a rite can improve the afterlife of any child who might die. The names given to Indian children are usually a mixture of Christian and ancient Indian names.

Marriages in Guatemala are made both by arrangement and by choice. In the case of arranged marriages, long negotiations

take place between the families of the girl and boy. Go-betweens are used during the bargaining, and astrologers may be consulted. Indian husbands are expected to pay a dowry, varying with their wealth, to the family of the bride. Normally, only men and women from the same village and the same tribe marry, but there are exceptions. Week-long celebrations involving entire villages take place after weddings and include elaborate feasting and dancing. Husbands are the heads of households, but wives are respected, for they prepare meals and help cultivate crops.

Indian dress is distinctive and attractive, little changed since the time when the Spaniards arrived. Women wear colorful headdresses, tunics, and skirts, and the men adorn themselves with richly patterned sashes, kerchiefs, hatbands, and tassels. Designs vary greatly, often from village to village. Because the Indians tend to be poor, the traditional outfits expensive, and denim cheap, many men are

Indian farmers often walk 10 or 20 miles to town on market days. Although non-Indian styles of dress have made some headway among the highland tribes, most Indians still prefer their traditional clothing.

These students are studying Spanish as part of the curriculum for majors in architecture at a private university in Guatemala City. Although Spanish is the official language, many Guatemalans grow up speaking Indian languages and must learn Spanish later in life in order to earn college degrees.

adopting Western dress in the villages. The women seem to be slower to change.

Non-Indians

Westernized Guatemalans, who make up about 60 percent of the population, lead a life very similar to that of citizens of other Latin American countries. Quite naturally, the Spanish influence on their customs is pronounced. Since Guatemala gained its independence from Spain many years ago, its culture has also been influenced by customs and technology from North America and European countries other than Spain. A visitor finds fewer differences between life in Guatemala City and everyday life in London, Madrid, or New York City than between life in Gua-

temala City and a rural Guatemalan Indian village.

Education

During the period of Spanish rule, almost all education in Guatemala was in the hands of the Catholic Church. During the colonial era, education was restricted largely to the sons of wealthier Spaniards and mestizos. A university was founded at Antigua in 1679, and the first classes were held two years later. However, it was not until after independence from Spain that there was any move to provide education for all Guatemalan children.

In 1875, the Guatemalan government recognized the principle that all school-age children should receive a compulsory, free

During Holy Week (the week before Easter) Guatemalan streets are lined with decorative "carpets" made of sand, sawdust, leaves, or flower petals. Here, young people fill a stencil with petals to lay one of several yellow designs on a green carpet of pine needles.

Photo by Dr. Roma Hoff

Courtesy of Museum of Modern Art of Latin America

A city street has become a carpet of flowers, but the design can be admired for only a short time. Processions will travel this route and destroy the intricate geometric pattern.

At an outdoor stand, fritters are cooking in oil. At other stands, tacos, enchiladas, colored sweet drinks, fruits, and cashew nuts are sold. Vendors of weavings, blankets, and jewelry often set up shop on the curbs of the city streets.

Photo by Dr. Roma Hoff

education. However, circumstances made this desirable goal impossible to attain. The government simply could not afford the expense of setting up a national educational system. Also, many parents in rural areas could not, and still cannot, understand why their children should spend time learning to read and write when they are needed to work in the fields to help their families.

During the late 1940s, the Arévalo government waged a campaign to end illiteracy. Unfortunately, the scheme had very little effect. Even today only an estimated 3 out of every 10 Guatemalans can read and write. Not unexpectedly, the most literate Guatemalans are those living in urban areas. In the most recent national census (1973), the illiteracy rate was found to range from a low of 28.2 percent in urban areas to a high of 68.6 percent in rural areas.

At present, there are both public and private schools in Guatemala. Owners of *fincas* (plantations) are required by law to provide schools for the children of their employees, but many of these schools are of substandard quality. Schools in cities and larger towns are better than those in rural areas, for the latter often lack equipment and teachers. The Guatemalan government is placing increasing emphasis on the need to improve the country's educational system.

Guatemala's Indians are a special problem, for many of them consider Spanish a

45

foreign language. Indian children must be taught Spanish before they can begin their education in earnest. Unfortunately, many Indian parents see no reason why their children should learn the language of the outsiders. It is also difficult for the government to find teachers who can speak an Indian dialect as well as Spanish.

The Guatemalan educational system has three levels: primary school, secondary and vocational school, and the university. Most students still attend only primary school, but more and more of them, particularly in the larger cities and towns, are now continuing their education. Gifted students can enter the University of San Carlos of Guatemala in Guatemala City.

The university, an autonomous body, has eight faculties: juridical and social sciences, medical sciences, chemistry and pharmacy, engineering, economics, dentistry, humanities, and agriculture.

Religion

The Roman Catholic faith is by far the most important religion in Guatemala, although there is complete religious freedom and non-Catholic missionaries are permitted in the country. There are small numbers of Protestants, Jews, and people of other faiths. The Roman Catholicism of the Westernized Guatemalans is similar to that practiced in other countries, but

Courtesy of Inter-American Development Bank

A librarian catalogs new books at Rafael Landívar University. Almost all of the the 32,000 volumes in this library were purchased from Spain, which has a highly developed publishing industry and markets many books, particularly in technical fields, to Spanish-speaking countries in the Americas.

Courtesy of Inter-American Development Bank

Future doctors walk across the campus of the medical school at Del Valle University in Guatemala City. With just slightly more than 1,250 doctors, 600 hospitals, and 100 dispensaries, Guatemala's need for trained medical personnel to care for its growing population has become a national priority.

Although the University of San Carlos was founded in 1679, recent expansions have given some sections of the campus a modern look. Students at this university are known for their political activism, usually on behalf of Guatemala's poor.

Roman Catholicism as interpreted by the Indians is rather different. Preconquest Mayan religious customs have survived to this day among the Indians and have been blended with Christianity. The Christian cross proved to be an acceptable religious symbol to the Indians, for the cross was an ancient Mayan symbol signifying the four directions. Christian saints were soon added to the roster of Indian gods, and even today Indians frequently pray to their old gods outside the village church and to the Christian God inside the church.

Throughout the year there are many religious festivals and pilgrimages. Indians pray in their churches for good crops of corn. They also hold celebrations to please the ancient corn spirit. Of the many pilgrimages, the pilgrimage to the Black Christ of Esquipulas is probably the most famous. Esquipulas is a small village not far from the point where Guatemala, Honduras, and El Salvador meet. In 1595, Catholic priests erected a wooden figure of Christ in the local chapel. Since the Indians heartily disliked the white conquerors, the priests had the five-foot-high figure coated with a brown-black pigment so that it resembled the skin tone of the Indians. Age and smoke have turned the Christ of Esquipulas black—which was also the color of the Mayan god Ek Ahau. The shrine was an instant success, and today thousands of people from Guatemala and other Central American countries visit it every year. Many of the sick who have prayed before the Black Christ have reported miraculous cures.

47

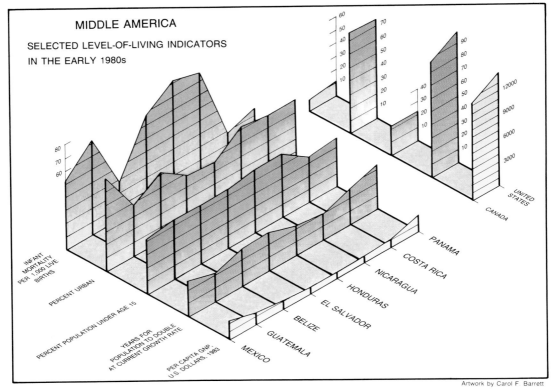

MIDDLE AMERICA

SELECTED LEVEL-OF-LIVING INDICATORS
IN THE EARLY 1980s

INFANT MORTALITY PER 1,000 LIVE BIRTHS

PERCENT URBAN

PERCENT POPULATION UNDER AGE 15

YEARS FOR POPULATION TO DOUBLE AT CURRENT GROWTH RATE

PER CAPITA GNP, U.S. DOLLARS, 1983

MEXICO
GUATEMALA
BELIZE
EL SALVADOR
HONDURAS
NICARAGUA
COSTA RICA
PANAMA
CANADA
UNITED STATES

Artwork by Carol F. Barrett

This graph shows how each of five factors, which are suggestive of the quality and style of life, varies among the eight Middle American countries. Canada and the United States are included for comparison. Data from "1986 World Population Data Sheet" (Washington, D.C.: Population Reference Bureau, Inc., 1986).

Literature

Although a small country, Guatemala has made several notable contributions to literature in Spanish. Enrique Gómez Carrillo (1873–1927) was known for the sophisticated outlook of his prose, while Miguel Ángel Asturias (1899–1974), author of a series of powerful novels—*El Presidente, Strong Wind,* and *Mulatto Woman,* among others—won the 1967 Nobel Prize in literature.

María Eulalia Antonio Pio weaves part of a *huipil,* a woman's garment of Indian design that has a head opening and hangs in triangles in front and back. Working in her home, she participates in a national program to develop and market high-quality textiles of indigenous design.

Courtesy of Inter-American Development Bank

A father and son, caught by a sudden rainstorm, ride near a cornfield just outside the village of Tecpán.

The instructor in a refresher course on delivering babies uses a doll for demonstration. In Indian communities, children are usually ushered into the world by midwives, not by doctors.

Photo by Dr. Roma Hoff

At the Hotel Antigua in Antigua, a marimba band entertains diners on a Sunday afternoon. The boy on the right has dressed up in his best suit to enjoy a good meal and the most popular form of music in the country.

Because Indians use the front vestibule of the church of Santo Tomás for their votive ceremonies, visitors must enter through a side door. This candle-lighting ceremony might accompany prayers for the cure of an ailing child or for the prosperity and well-being of a couple soon to be married.

Photo by Dr. Roma Hoff

Children of Guatemala belong to warm and affectionate families and frequently have the advantage of a grandparent living in their home, a source of wise counsel over the years.

Arts and Crafts

Before the coming of the Spanish conquerors, the Indians of Guatemala produced pottery, clothing, and other necessities. Today, Indian communities are still largely self-sustaining. In order to provide needed income, however, Indians often sell their craft products. Foremost is the Indian pottery. The ancient Maya made beautiful decorated pieces, but modern Guatemalan Indians produce only simple pots and water jars. Among the other craftwares sold are baskets, decorated gourds, costume jewels, woven mats to cover floors and walls, and a variety of textile products. Using hand- and foot-looms and natural dyes, the Indians produce blankets and articles of clothing for personal use and sale to tourists and non-Indian Guatemalans. In recent times, larger and larger quantities of Western-style goods have been reaching the country villages, and they have slowly been taking the place of some products of Indian arts and crafts.

Sports and Recreation

A diversity of terrain and cultural influences has encouraged in Guatemala a number of sports and recreations. The numerous volcanoes in the country are a challenge to the amateur hiker, although the peaks require no technical mountaineering skills. Views from the tops of the volcanoes are superb on clear days, and it is usually possible to descend into the dormant craters after climbing to the summit.

Many tasty varieties of fish can be

These schoolboys are supposed to be lining up for morning calisthenics. Exercise, fitness, personal hygiene, and nutrition are important subjects in Guatemalan schools.

caught in Guatemala's mountain streams. Deep-sea fishermen catch barracuda, sailfish, and other varieties in both the Atlantic and Pacific oceans.

The most popular games played in Guatemala come from Europe and North America. Soccer is played everywhere, and thousands of spectators flock to important contests. Basketball and baseball are also widely played. Bicycle races are frequent, and the more important racers tour the major cities and towns of the country. Other sports are golf, tennis, horseback riding, and horse racing.

Aura Estela Echevarría's family rebuilt their home near Chimaltenango after their old house was destroyed in an earthquake in 1976. The new house is made mostly of concrete blocks, which are more quake-resistant than the traditional adobe blocks. Corrugated iron roofing is used instead of the heavy red tiles that caused many deaths when they fell during the quake.

César Franco (*left*) discusses insect damage and soil deficiencies affecting his onion crop with Ricardo Cojulún González, an extension agent of the national government. Franco, a former sharecropper, now owns his 10-acre farm, thanks to government loans that enabled him to purchase the land.

4) The Economy

Guatemala's economy is relatively weak and very vulnerable to worldwide fluctuations in prices of agricultural goods. It is also a very uneven economy; most of the wealth is in the hands of a few, while most Guatemalans barely participate in the nation's organized system of commerce, hold no bank accounts, and have no access to credit.

Over nearly five centuries, Guatemalan governments—despite sometimes good intentions—have made little progress in promoting economic justice. A few wealthy Guatemalans, in league with foreign entrepreneurs, still effectively manage the nation's business.

Belatedly, the government has moved into the economic sphere. Responding to pressure from international lenders, especially the World Bank, the government has created housing and sanitation authorities, as well as agencies to oversee the production and distribution of electric power and to cope with accelerated urbanization. A devastating earthquake in 1976 brought about the creation of several governmental agencies that now provide agricultural extension services and sources of credit to rural Guatemalans to help them rebuild.

Despite recent progress, Guatemala still has two economic systems largely separate from each other. One is the modern sector—wealthy landowners who produce the bulk of the nation's major commodity exports and a growing number of foreign and domestic industrial entrepreneurs based near Guatemala City. The other is a backward sector that includes the majority of Guatemala's work force—Indians farming small tracts of land, mostly in the western highlands.

Many of these Indians spend their lives working small fields of maize, beans, and wheat. All of these crops are grown for consumption in Guatemala. The plots of ground farmed by Indians often cling to the sides of steep hills. Plows are seldom used to cultivate the soil; instead the Indian farmer uses a machete (a long knife) to chop down weeds and a hoe to dig up the ground. Each step in the growing cycle is accompanied by prayers, incense burning, and the sacrifice of chickens.

Guatemalan Indians are usually not subsistence farmers, as are the peasants in many other underdeveloped countries who live on the food they grow and occasionally barter for other goods. In Guatemala, Indians who produce a surplus usually sell it; those who do not produce enough food often seek jobs on coffee plantations or sell craft products at village markets.

Agriculture

Farming employs well over half of Guatemala's work force but accounts for only about one-quarter of the gross national

Indians put their wheat harvest through a thresher that draws its power from a tractor's engine. Even though this method may look old-fashioned, it is highly practical in Guatemala's rugged terrain, where large threshing machines built for level land cannot operate.

The effectiveness of water filters can mean the difference between sickness and health for many Guatemalans. Ways of removing contaminants from drinking water are tested at the Central American Institute for Research and Industrial Technology in Guatemala City.

product. Most agricultural production is concentrated on large plantations. Ninety percent of Guatemala's coffee, for example, is grown on only 10 percent of the country's 37,000 coffee plantations. With government assistance, operators of large plantations are steadily increasing their yield of coffee per acre, while small producers fall farther and farther behind.

Coffee, which accounts for about one-third of Guatemala's export earnings, is grown mostly in the Pacific Piedmont region in rich volcanic soils at elevations of 1,000 feet to 5,000 feet. Lower down or on poorer soils, cotton, Guatemala's second most important export crop, is grown. Sugarcane plantations exist as well, mainly on the Pacific coastal lowlands.

Banana production is concentrated in the Caribbean and Pacific lowlands, on large plantations operated by foreign-owned companies. Guatemala's banana production was initially developed by the United Fruit Company around the beginning of the twentieth century. Although working conditions on United Fruit's plantations were better than those provided by Guatemalan-owned agribusinesses, many Guatemalans have long resented foreign-owned companies as a symbol of U.S. domination of their economy. The United Fruit

A farmer of Zacapa department east of Guatemala City sprays his onion crop to kill insects and to prevent fungus disease. This level area of Guatemala produces several crops, including okra and melons, for export to the United States.

Company was also a powerful factor in Guatemalan politics. United Fruit sold its Guatemalan holdings to another U.S. multinational company, Del Monte, in 1972.

The operation of large plantations is costly. Growing bananas, for example, requires large outlays for research and development and to ensure that the mature fruit reaches overseas markets on an extremely tight schedule. Adverse weather can also prove costly to a banana plantation; bananas are grown on moist lowlands where there must be both enough rainfall and good drainage. The hurricane winds that are common in these areas often ravage the crop.

All of the major commodity crops require much hand labor, which is plentiful and cheap in Guatemala. Coffee, for example, is a sensitive crop that can only be harvested by hand. Coffee trees require a lot of careful cultivation as well during the five years they need to mature. About six months after a grown tree's white blossoms fall, coffee cherries begin to appear in clusters. When the cherries develop a crimson hue, they are ready to be picked by hand, and the coffee beans inside the cherries are removed and laid out to dry.

This requires a lot of labor, which is provided by Guatemalans willing to work long hours for low wages, sometimes for less than half the minimum wage—which itself is less than $3 a day in rural areas.

Many of those who help cultivate and harvest the nation's coffee, cotton, sugar, and banana crops can find only seasonal employment. Although in 1983 Guatemala's per capita annual income stood at about $1,200, this figure is an average that hardly reflects what most Guatemalans earn. Guatemala's president at that time, José Efraín Ríos Montt, estimated that, of some 7.5 million Guatemalans, 3 million had incomes of less than $200 a year and 2.5 million had incomes of less than $450.

The Indians of the highlands make up the largest group of Guatemalans engaged in agriculture. The corn, beans, and wheat that they cultivate on small parcels of land is mostly for local consumption. The raising of these crops and their marketing creates in the villages what one anthropologist has termed "penny capitalism," a small-scale free-enterprise system separate from the overall national economy. Each village serves as the commercial center for the outlying highlands.

In addition to providing a marketplace

Courtesy of Inter-American Development Bank

Francisco de Léon measures the moisture content of corn in a new type of solar grain drier. Many farmers have traditionally dried grains and beans by using the heat of the sun, but to do so they had to spread their produce out on patios or on the ground. Every time rain came, the drying harvest had to be taken in to avoid spoilage. This new enclosed system should make safer use of the same energy resource.

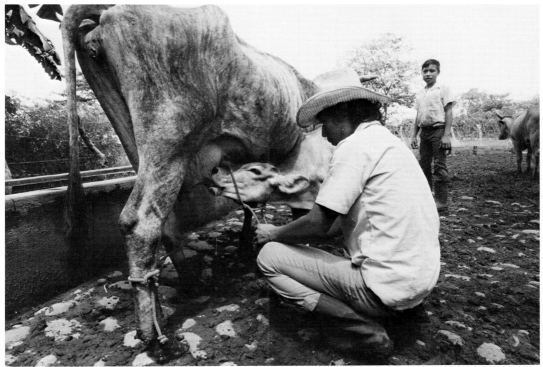

Once her calf has had its fill, this cow on a farm near Montufar will be milked by hand. Because of an abundant supply of local labor, Guatemalan farms have been slow to mechanize.

for crops, each village supports necessary merchants and craftspersons, including makers of farm implements and of earthen cooking vessels, plates, and cups. In most villages, local buyers and visitors can also find handmade shoes, hats, and many other items of clothing. Each village, with its own local upper class of resident businesspersons, is a microcosm of the nation as a whole.

On a national level, Guatemala's earnings are greatly affected by ups and downs in world commodity prices. In the 1980s there were more downs than ups. The nation was also hit hard in the 1970s by drastic increases in the price of imported petroleum. On a village level, the conflict between guerrillas and government forces has resulted in a sharp drop in tourism, long a major source of revenue in rural Guatemala.

Livestock

Cattle raising has become economically important to Guatemala in recent years as the country's production of milk, meat, and hides has increased. Ranches tend to be large and are located mostly in the Pacific coastal area, particularly in the department of Escuintla. In 1980 Guatemala had an estimated 1.5 million head of cattle; livestock represented about 30 percent of the value of the production of the agricultural sector.

In the highlands, poor farmers are raising more pigs and poultry, and in the western highlands, the raising of sheep and goats is on the increase.

Forestry

Belatedly, Guatemalan authorities have become concerned about the uncontrolled cutting of the nation's forests. Between 1950 and 1980, some 30 to 50 percent of Guatemala's forests were cut down. Experts estimated that 90 percent of all wood cut in Guatemala is used as firewood for cooking by highland Indians, for whom firewood is the main source of energy.

Guatemala has sought outside investment and help in maintaining its still-considerable forests and in exploiting such valuable forest products as chicle (the base for chewing gum), vanilla, sarsaparilla, camphor, cinnamon, and medicinal barks and herbs.

Fishing

Guatemala is trying to develop commercial fishing along its Pacific coast. The waters there abound in shrimp, tuna, snap-per, and mackerel—which so far account for less than 1 percent of the nation's overall production of food. Most of this production from the ocean is exported, even though fish could provide much-needed protein in Guatemala's diet.

Mining and Manufacturing

To date, mining has contributed little to the economy, although Guatemala has sizable deposits of nickel, copper, antimony, zinc, tin, lead, and tungsten. A copper mine in Alta Verapaz produces some 12,000 tons of copper annually. Sharp drops in the world price of nickel caused the country's only major nickel mine, north of Lake Izabal, to shut down.

Although its industrial base is still underdeveloped, Guatemala is seeking to

Photo by Dr. Roma Hoff

The clothes of the Indians in Antigua's market are as colorful as their baskets and sacks. In recent years, many Indians have foregone their native dress, whereas once there were more than 200 distinctive tribal costumes in the country.

Fresh shrimp are transported in refrigerated trucks from the Pacific coast to Guatemala City, where workers at Refrigerated Products of Guatemala pack them for an even longer journey—to the United States by jet airplane.

The straight board on the left was properly dried and cured; the warped one on the right was not. Drying techniques studied by researchers such as Jaime Valladares can increase the usefulness of Guatemala's forest resources.

After the earthquake of 1976, many countries "adopted" damaged cities to help them rebuild. Norway's Red Cross worked with Patzún, as a large sign declares. Other participating countries were Canada, France, Spain, and Nicaragua.

The rubber sheeting made at this factory in Guatemala City will be used in manufacturing shoe soles and heels.

increase its industrial output. Manufacturing continues to be concentrated in Guatemala City, where the most important industries involve the processing of food and production of beverages—mostly for domestic consumption. In addition, there are plants manufacturing textiles, construction materials, pharmaceuticals, and rubber, paper, and electrical products. Local industries, protected by tariffs and encouraged by tax incentives, are making an increasing amount of the goods that Guatemala consumes.

Within Guatemala City, there is an amazing array of small shops and home-based enterprises producing materials for neighborhood and community markets. This includes everything from shoes and clothing to metal products and automotive batteries. More than two-thirds of those engaged in manufacturing in Guatemala work at establishments employing four or fewer workers.

Transportation and Communications

Fewer than 2,000 of Guatemala's 11,000 miles of road are paved. Trunk highways cross the nation from coast to coast via Guatemala City, and two trunk highways extend from the Mexican border to the Salvadoran frontier. One of these, the Pacific Highway, serves the fertile coastal plain, and the other, the Pan-American Highway, runs through the highlands and Guatemala City. About 200,000 motor vehicles are registered.

The main railway system, the Ferrocarriles de Guatemala, is government-owned and has just over 500 miles of rail. A government-owned airline, Aviateca,

Bulldozers are often required to move mountains when roads are built through Guatemala's rugged high country. The road being constructed here is now open, linking Cuilapa and Chiquimulilla.

furnishes both domestic and international service.

Guatemala has about 70 radio broadcasting stations and four commercial television channels, plus one government TV station. There are eight daily newspapers.

Energy

With financial assistance from such international agencies as the Inter-American Development Bank, Guatemala is increasing its output of electrical energy, particularly through the construction of hydroelectric power facilities. In the early 1980s, foreign oil companies developed reserves discovered at Rubelsanto, in Alta Verapaz department, and constructed a pipeline more than 100 miles long to convey it to the Caribbean port of Santo Tomás de Castilla. The country has one small refinery at Escuintla, which is operated by Texaco.

Financial Position

Until recently, Guatemala always had monetary reserves large enough to support the value of its currency. But after 1981, adverse conditions in the international market for its most important exports were complicated by the renewal of social and political tensions in the region. Subsequently, Guatemala's balance of

Sewer lines and a storm drainage system are being installed in Colonia la Florida, a poor area of Guatemala City. They will replace the unsanitary gutter—visible as a weedy depression at left—down which garbage and raw sewage used to flow.

61

In the village of San Antonio on Lake Atitlán, a young man wears the typical shirt of the town and sells other shirts of the same design. Although such a shirt might cost $25 in the United States, the price is only about $5 here. The young man's business is a small-scale example of the enterprises that can spring up around Guatemala's tourist attractions. As the country's political climate stabilizes, Guatemala should be able to attract more visitors.

Photo by Dr. Roma Hoff

Courtesy of Museum of Modern Art of Latin America

Among Indian women, such daily chores as doing the family laundry are social events, as here on the shore of Lake Atitlán.

Among Indians of the Guatemalan highlands, firewood is the most commonly used source of energy for cooking and heating. Widespread use of firewood has led to the deforestation of many areas, and Indians of today must often pay high prices for wood in their local markets or travel long distances to gather it themselves.

Smoke from burning copal—an incense made of tree resin—drifts out of the vestibule of the church of Santo Tomás in Chichicastenango, where the incense accompanies the prayers of worshippers from many highland villages.

payments became negative, and it became a debtor nation. Estimates indicate that, by the end of 1986, the external resources gap could reach $160 million. As a result, imports are being restricted and production is being decreased, leading to a drastic rise in the rates of unemployment and underemployment.

The Future

Looking ahead, Guatemalans are hopeful that the restoration of domestic tranquillity may allow the flagging tourism industry to expand again. Besides the country's great natural beauty and its Mayan treasures, Guatemala offers a rare chance to see Indian people living much as they have for centuries. Continued efforts to develop fishing and light industry promise further economic gains.

Index